TEDDY'S

Picture Word·Book

Words

Dee Turner

Pictures

Lyn Mitchell

Ladybird

pyjamas
window
bed
pillow
slippers
alarm clock
picture
I get up early.
light
blind
drawer
duvet
cupboard
curtains

skirt
jumper
sweatshirt
shorts
We get dressed.
tights
jeans
pants
shoes
dress
socks
trousers
t-shirt
trainers
coat
jacket

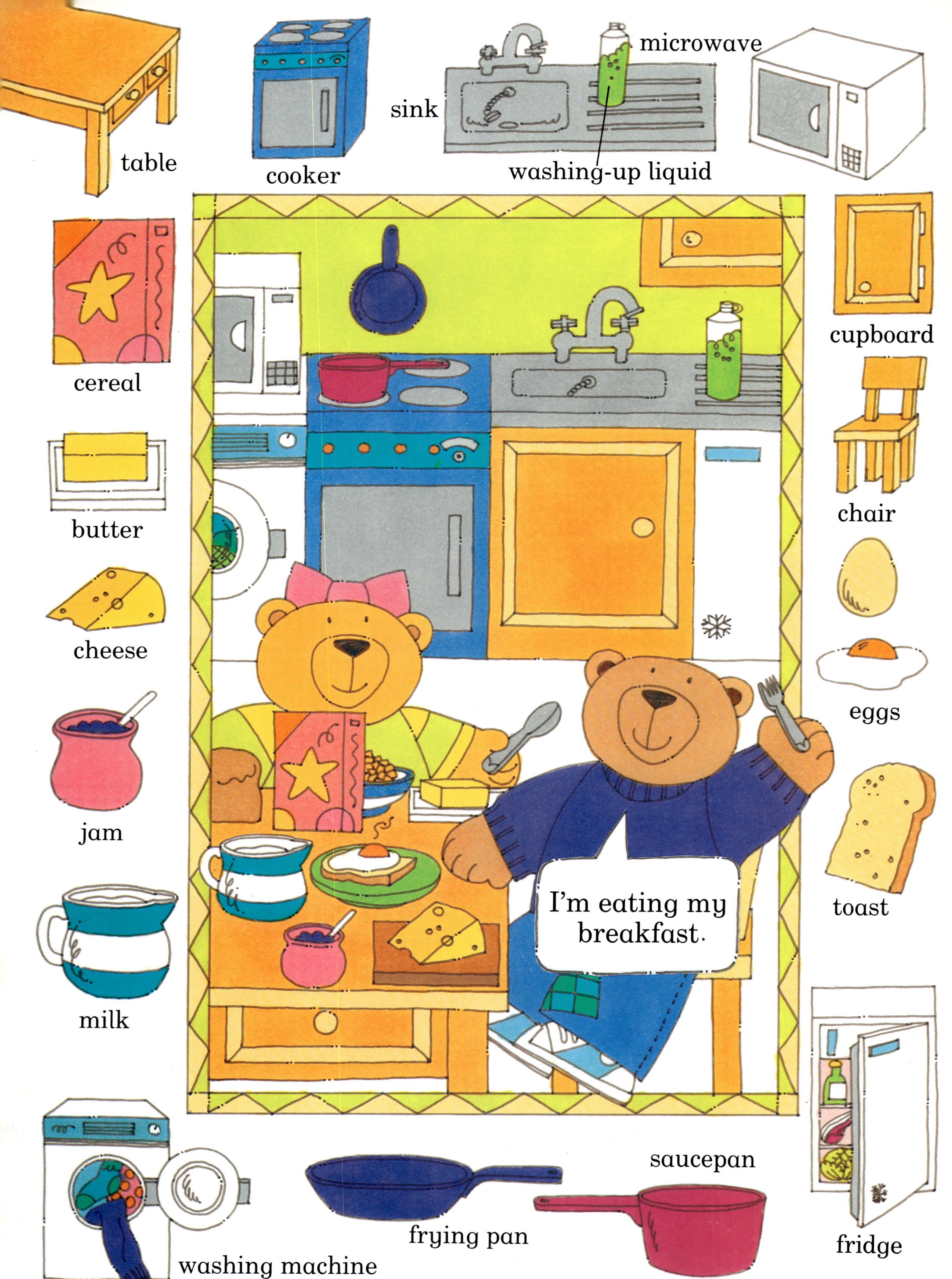
table
cooker
sink
microwave
washing-up liquid
cereal
cupboard
chair
butter
cheese
eggs
jam
I'm eating my breakfast.
toast
milk
saucepan
frying pan
fridge
washing machine

cloud
rainbow
snowflake
thunder and lightning
kite
snow
wind
We like looking out of the window.
hail
sunshine
raindrop
blue sky
rain
storm
puddle
sun

houses
shop
pavement
road
roof
streetlight
chimney
garden
children
I'm going for a walk.
traffic light
buggy
car
gate
fence
bicycle

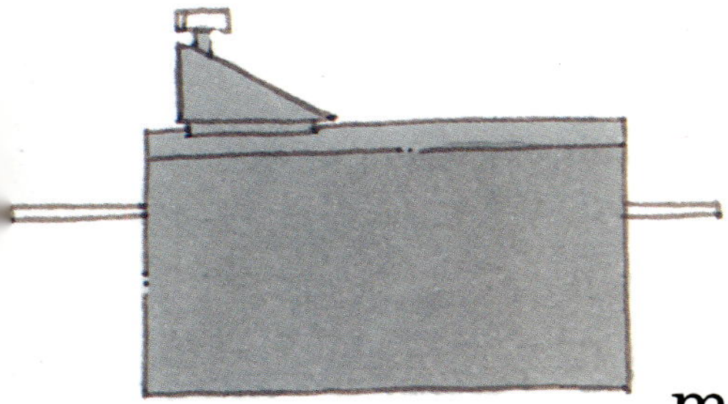

checkout

money

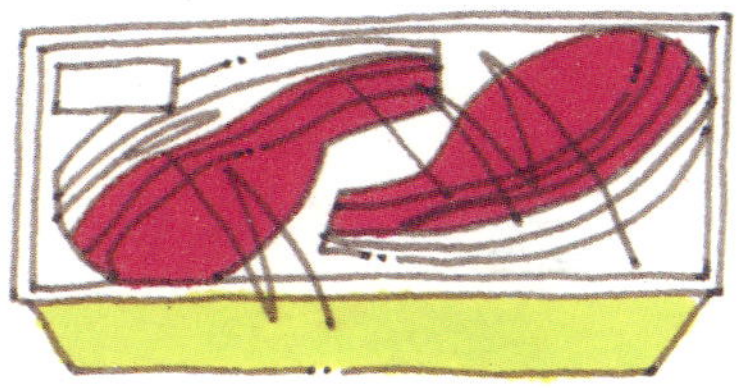

meat

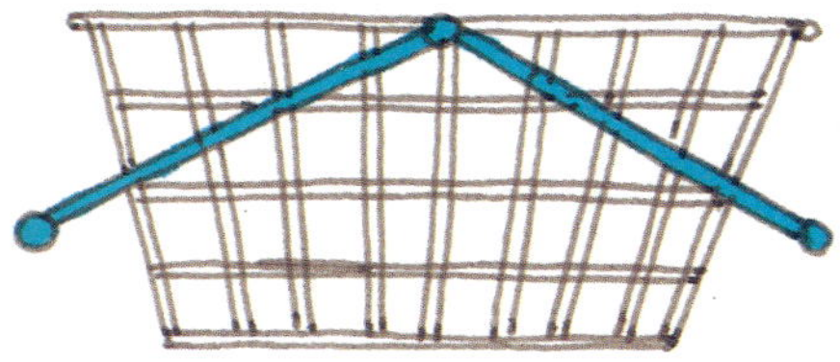

basket

fruit juice

sweets

magazine

cereal

biscuits

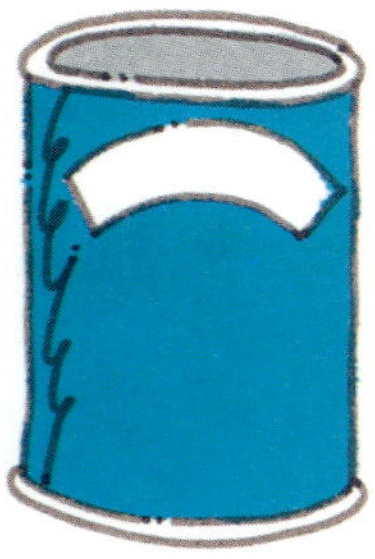

tin

pet food

trolley

supermarket

till

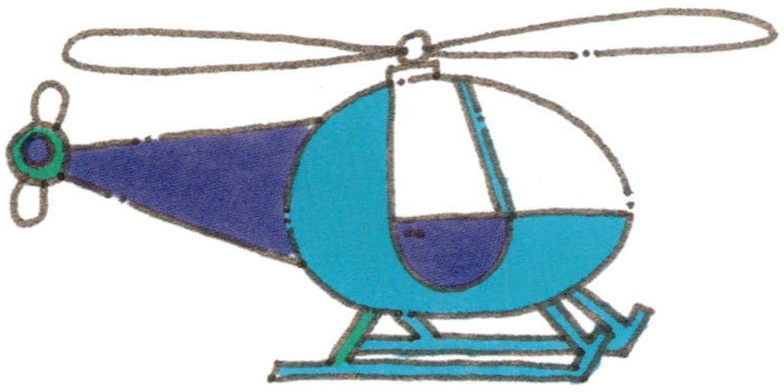
helicopter

jumbo jet

control tower

satellite dish

radar

bird

hot air balloon

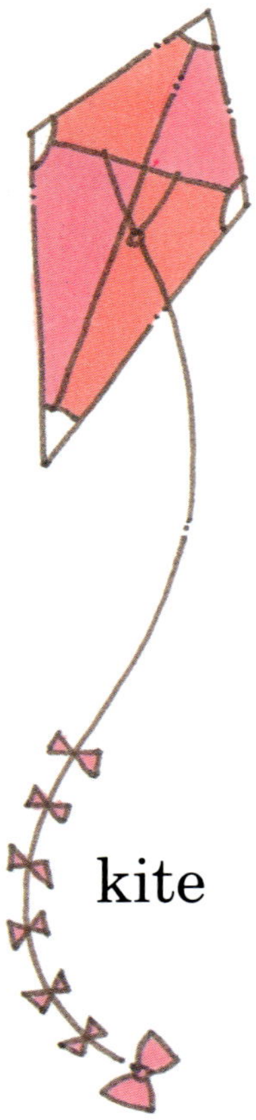
kite

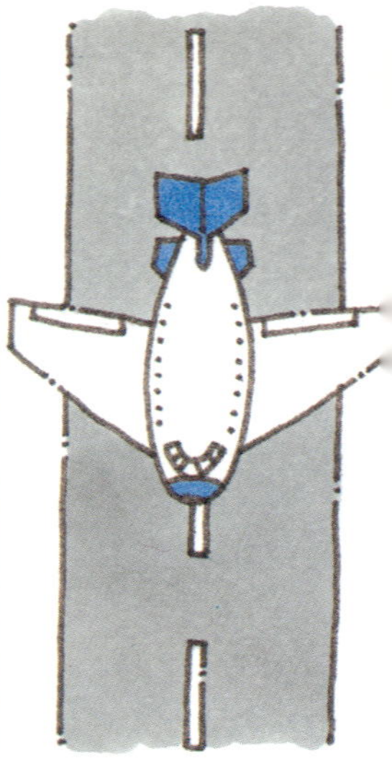
runway

airport

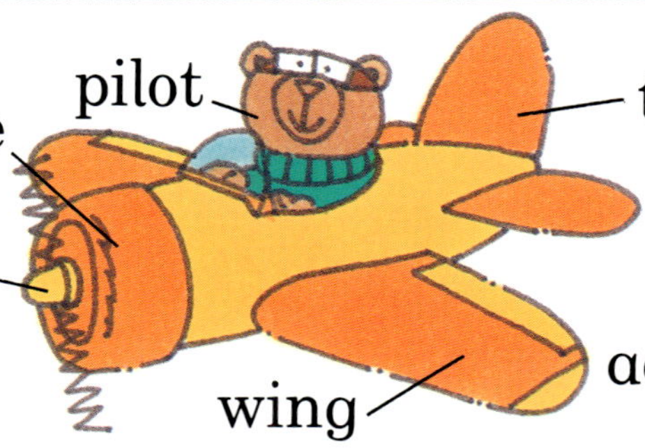

aeroplane

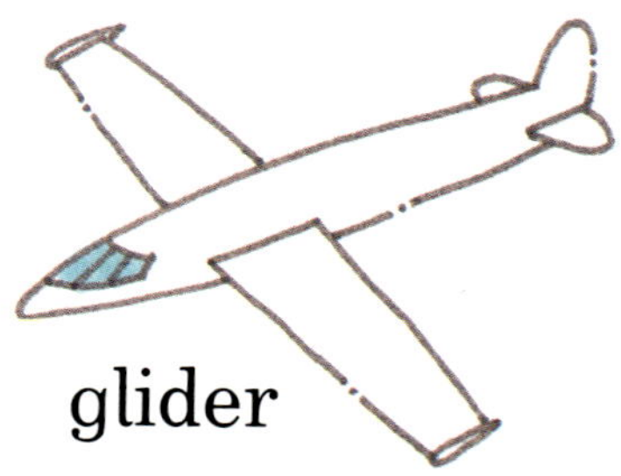
glider

syringe
ointment
height chart
eye test chart
bandage
stethoscope
I'm seeing the doctor.
medicine
tablets
hermometer
nurse
scales
doctor's bag
doctor

farm
tractor
trailer
hills
chicken
farmer
combine harvester
dog
duck
field
I'm feeding the animals.
cow
pig
sheep
horse

train set
doll's house
monster
I'm playing with my toys.
tape recorder
building bricks
skipping rope
ball
robot
spaceship
doll
teddy bear
jigsaw
toy farm

calculator

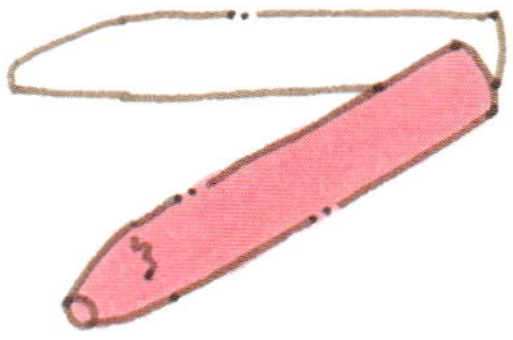

chalk

alphabet chart

poster

clay

paintbrush

blackboard

computer

drawing pin

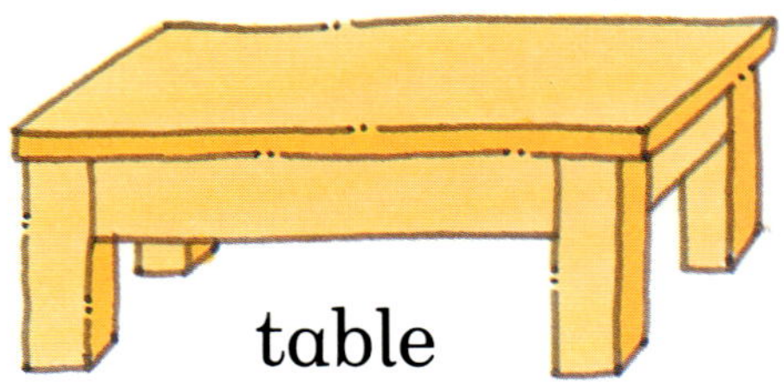

table

paper
coat peg
lunch box
plasticine
scissors
glue
workbook
I'm reading to my friend.
teacher
school bag
pencil
pen
paint pot

spaghetti
cake
biscuits
meat
orange juice
fork
knife
crisps
apple
orange
spoon
ice cream
I'm eating my lunch.
milkshake
bananas
chips
sandwich
plate
pizza
bowl

pink
rainbow
yellow
white
green
orange
grey
I like bright colours.
purple
red
black
brown
blue

circle
triangle
square
rectangle
star
0
nought
1
one
2
two
3
three
4
four
5
five
6
six
7
seven
8
eight
9
nine
10
ten
I know lots of numbers.

carpet
video recorder
radiator
lampshade
television
video
screen
clock
switch
newspaper
THE TIMES
I'm watching television.
cushion
comic
sofa
armchair
rug

lion
elephant
crocodile
ostrich
giraffe
monkey
kangaroo
camel
I like my toy animals.
tiger
panda
snake
shark
octopus
zebra
hippopotamus
polar bear

present
straws
party squeaker
party dress
paper cup
jelly
balloons
party hats
streamers
It's my birthday.
paper plates
birthday cake
birthday cards
candles
chocolate biscuits

watering can
sandpit
bucket
bird's nest
tree house
Let's play in the garden.
rope ladder
bush
flowers
hosepipe
butterfly
spade
snail
bee
wheelbarrow
climbing frame
lawn mower

toothbrush
toothpaste
towel
washbasin
dressing gown
tap
mirror
toilet paper
bubble bath
laundry basket
shampoo
soap
I like having a bath.
water
bath
mat
sponge
toilet

giant

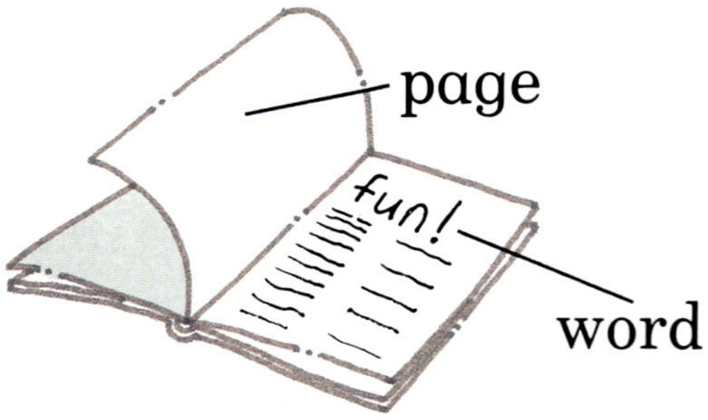

dragon

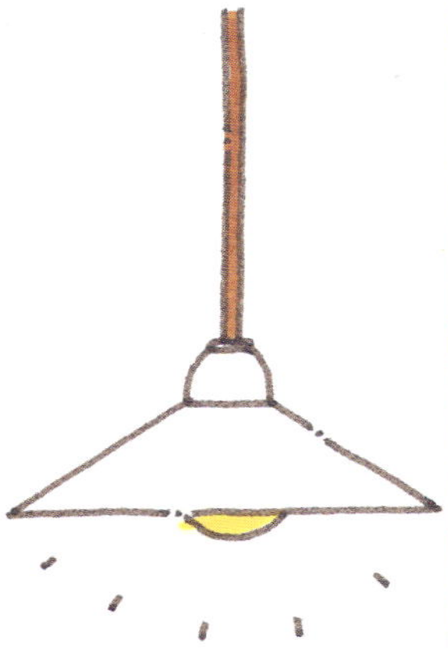
light

comic

magician

picture

storybook

bookshelf

ghost

castle

yawning

stars

sleeping

moon

owl

moth

cat

dreaming

lamp

streetlight

bat

Word list

aeroplane
airport
alarm clock
alphabet
apple
armchair

ball
balloons
bananas
bandage
basket
bat
bath
bathroom
bed
bedroom
bedtime
bee
bicycle
bird
bird's nest
birthday cake
birthday cards
birthday party
biscuits
black
blackboard
blind
blue
bookshelf
bowl
brown
bubble bath
bucket
buggy
building bricks
bush
butter
butterfly

cake
calculator
camel
candles
car
carpet
castle
cat
cereal
chair
chalk
chart
checkout
cheese
chicken
children
chimney
chips
chocolate biscuits
circle
clay
climbing frame
clock
clothes
cloud
coat
coat peg
colours
combine harvester
comic
computer
control tower
cooker
cow
crisps
crocodile
cupboard
curtains
cushion

doctor
doctor's bag
dog
doll
doll's house
dragon
drawer
drawing pin
dreaming
dress
dressing gown
duck
duvet

eggs
eight
elephant
engine
eye test chart

farm
farmer
fence
field
five
flowers
flying
food
fork
four
fridge
fruit juice
frying pan

garden
gate
ghost
giant
giraffe
glider
glue
green
grey

hail
height chart
helicopter
hills
hippopotamus
horse
hosepipe
hot air balloon
houses

ice cream

jacket
jam
jeans
jelly
jigsaw
jumbo jet
jumper

kangaroo
kitchen
kite
knife

lamp
lampshade
laundry basket
lawn mower
light
lion
lunch box

magazine
magician
mat
meat
medicine
microwave
milk
milkshake
mirror
money
monkey
monster
moon
moth

newspaper
nine
nose
nought
numbers
nurse

octopus
ointment
one
orange
orange juice
ostrich
owl

page
paint pot
paintbrush
panda
pants
paper
paper cup
paper plates
party dress
party hats
party squeaker
pavement
pen
pencil
pet food
picture
pig
pillow
pilot
pink
pizza
plasticine
plate
polar bear
poster
present
puddle
purple
pyjamas

radar
radiator
rain
rainbow
raindrop
rectangle
red
road
robot
roof
rope ladder
rug
runway

sandpit
sandwich
satellite dish
saucepan
scales
school
school bag
scissors
screen
seven
shampoo
shapes
shark
sheep
shoes
shop
shopping
shorts
sink
sitting room
six
skipping rope
skirt
sky
sleeping
slippers
snail
snake
snow
snowflake
soap
socks
sofa
spaceship
spade
spaghetti
sponge
spoon
square
star
stars
stethoscope
storm
storybook
storytime
straws
streamers
street
streetlight
sun
sunshine
supermarket
sweatshirt
sweets
switch
syringe

t-shirt
table
tablets
tail
tap
tape recorder
teacher
teddy bear
television
ten
thermometer
three
thunder and lightning
tiger
tights
till
tin
toast
toilet
toilet paper
toothbrush
toothpaste
towel
toys
toy farm
tractor
traffic light
trailer
train set
trainers
tree house
triangle
trolley
trousers
two

video
video recorder

washbasin
washing machine
washing-up liquid
water
watering can
weather
wheelbarrow
white
wild animals
wind
window
wing
word
workbook

yawning
yellow

zebra

A Times Four Book

Created by Times Four Publishing Ltd
5 High Street, Cuckfield, Sussex, RH17 5EN

Editor Dee Turner
Art Director Tony Potter

Typeset by Amber Graphics, Burgess Hill
Printed by Eastern Printing, Thailand

First published in the UK 1992 by Ladybird Books Ltd

BRITISH LIBRARY CATALOGUING IN PUBLICATION DATA
A catalogue record for this book is available from the British Library.

ISBN 0 7214 7550 7